Building Blocks for Library Space

Functional Guidelines

**The American Library Association
Library Administration and Management Association:
Buildings and Equipment Section
Functional Space Requirements Committee
Chicago 1995**

This is a working paper intended for use and feedback. Please send comments
and suggestions on use of or revisions to *Guidelines* to:

Functional Space Requirements Committee
c/o LAMA BES
American Library Association
50 E. Huron St.
Chicago, IL 60611

Edited by Deborah Bloomfield Dancik and Emelie Jensen Shroder
CAD illustrations by Michaels Associates and Hidell Architects
Shelving matrix by Anders Dahlgren

ISBN 0-8389-7746-4

The editors wish to thank their respective institutions for library time allowed
for editing and word processing this document:

Deborah Bloomfield Dancik, University of Alberta, Edmonton, Canada
Emelie Jensen Shroder, Chicago Public Library

Contents

ACKNOWLEDGMENTS

The committee extends sincere thanks to members of the library building consultants community, particularly the Active Building Consultants group, who have provided professional and technical advice, ideas on the structure and use of this publication, and dedication in bringing the project to fruition. Special appreciation to Andrea Michaels, David Michaels, Frank Hemphill, Nancy McAdams, and Nolan Lushington. Many committee members have contributed their energy and knowledge over the gestation of these Guidelines; in particular, Gloria Novak must be credited with the vision for initiating the project and moving the idea into reality.

Committee members since 1986:

Carol L. Anderson	Helmut Hutter	Emelie J. Shroder
Deborah B. Babel	Florence M. Mason	Matthew J. Simon
Joseph W. Barnes	David L. Michaels	Charles R. Smith
Anders Dahlgren	David C. Milling	Dennis E. Smith
Deborah B. Dancik	Annette M. Milliron	Lynn R. Smith
Mary Dale Deacon	Dale S. Montanelli	Donald G. Sweet
Ruth Ann Fraley	Arthur P. Morgan	Lamar Veatch
Mary M. Gilles	Richard W. Murphy	Stanley J. Wilder
Merri A. Hartse	Gloria J. Novak	Julia A. Woods
H. Harrison Heath	Karen A. Nuckolls	Janice Skinner Yeager
William Hidell	Sheryl B. Owens	Michael Ann Zemon
Edgar L. Hillsman	Walter W. Pennington	
Anne S. Hudson	Pal V. Rao	

Background and Intent

Experience in libraries has shown that in planning physical space requirements, the circulation space around or adjacent to an item (space for people to move around, stand, or sit in front of, or to otherwise use equipment and furniture) has been greatly underestimated or frequently ignored, making the total space much less functional. This is a working paper, both in terms of the number and range of items included and of the feet/meters recommended. The areas given in this document are based on intensive discussions among practicing librarians, architects, and professional building consultants to determine the typical size of a given item, e.g., a piece of furniture or equipment.

The square feet/square meters required, as given in the Guidelines, is an aggregate figure of the actual footprint (exact amount of space occupied) of an item *plus circulation area.* The committee determined that not giving the actual footprint size would remove the preoccupation with the footprint itself and aid library planners in focusing on the total space required (refer to the drawing of the atlas stand, Illustration 2, as an example of this approach). Space estimates are based on typical or average-sized furniture and equipment, not specific manufacturers' specifications. If much larger- or smaller-than-typical sizes are needed, then some adjustment in the totals will be necessary.

Each library's equipment and furniture needs differ. The functions, areas, and items listed are intended as building blocks. Users of the Guidelines should, by selecting those areas and items needed, determine the *workable* space required. But the totals are not the final answer to how big any particular library should be. The figures do not presume placement; various placements of items may provide economies of space, e.g., OPAC stations that are back-to-back versus in a line versus standalones. Nor are placement clearances and aisle widths included. The list is not intended as a checklist of all areas that could or should be included in a typical library.

These are guidelines, not standards or specifications, and given factors of scale, are most appropriately used in the planning of small to medium-sized libraries. They should be used in conjunction with existing standards, such as the Americans with Disabilities Act. Applicable state, local, and institutional codes or laws should be consulted. Also, professional associations, such as the Association for Educational Communications and Technology, publish program standards for specific types of libraries. A checklist, such as the *Checklist of Building Design Considerations*, and the bibliography *Planning Library Buildings: A Select Bibliography* (both available through ALA) can provide assistance.

Recent Changes Affecting Planning

Library-planning literature written prior to 1994 generally does not reflect the need for considerable technological space and configurations. The heavy emphasis on terminals, visuals, and displays, services now available and promoted by most libraries, is not adequately represented in the earlier program-planning literature. Thus, space estimates are found to be inadequate when the space constructed is actually used. Books and paper collections coexist with technologies, rather than being replaced by them, and the totality does not fit into the same space, nor is the space required for one interchangeable with that required for the other. Many states still use 75% net-to-gross space estimates to address the space required for electrical and telecommunications closets. Unfortunately, in the automated environment of current libraries, this can be insufficient. The new ADA requirements for additional traffic space also affect the total space needs to be considered.

Building Blocks will provide net space (assignable, usable, programmed space). For a complete building program, the unassigned (unprogrammed) space (net to gross) must be added to the program after the total programmed space ("assigned space," "usable area") is developed. Unassigned space includes the vestibule, lobby, public stairs, restrooms, fire stairs, major corridors, elevators, janitor's closets, pipe and duct spaces, mechanical and electrical rooms, etc., and is added as a percentage of the total building square footage.

For a smaller building (under 40,000 square feet), 25% net to gross may be adequate; for a medium-sized building (41,000–60,000 square feet), use 25%–30%; for a large building (100,000 square feet plus) or a renovation of any size, 30%–35% net to gross may be required. With a building renovation, space is frequently lost because of inefficiencies. The actual net to gross may also vary according to architectural decisions or the size of the entrance or any grand open spaces in the architectural design, since all of these spaces are unassigned (unprogrammed) space.

Projecting Total Area Requirement

To determine the square footage required for a specific library facility, find the sum (A) of the areas for *all assigned individual items, tasks, and rooms*. Then to (A) add an additional factor (B) of 33 1/3% for *unassignable areas* such as restrooms, mechanical and electrical rooms, elevators and stairs, vestibules, life/safety appurtenances, public telephones, drinking fountains, and wall thicknesses. The total (C) is the *gross square footage* required.[*] For example:

Total of all items, assignable spaces and services	(A) 30,000 sq. ft.
Net-to-gross factor (A) x 33 1/3% =	(B) +10,000 sq. ft.
Gross square footage	(C) 40,000 sq. ft.

Why 33 1/3%? It is the reciprocal of a commonly used net-to-gross factor of 75%. If it were determined that a library of 40,000 square feet was to be constructed, to find the net assignable area available for library use including aisles and corridors, one would typically use a 75% net-to-gross factor.

Gross square footage	(C) 40,000 sq. ft.
Net assignable square area (C) x 75% =	(A) 30,000 sq. ft.

---

[*] *Note:* If the facility is large (75,000 square feet or more) adding a factor of 15% of net (A) is advisable for the accommodation of corridors and larger main aisles.

Programmers, library directors and library boards, and university and municipal administrators should not be surprised if the program indicates a space increase of 300%. Often doubling the existing areas only brings existing capacities for customers, staff, and collections into compliance with current codes. Doubling existing space may not provide for growth or for change in service deliveries. If further expansion is suggested but not affordable, then review the needs of customers and staff and modify the library mission *and* revise the program to include planning for a second phase of expansion. It is essential that everyone involved in the planning and funding is assured that the facility will meet the intended program.

The facility's program must reflect the library's changing needs and constituencies. In an electronic library, paper-based collections may not grow at the same rate as in the past, but the addition of electronic technologies may increase the need for more staff and new service centers. Limited growth in some departments may be indicated even as more services are offered outside the facility itself. And as barrier-free accessibility brings more disabled customers into the large community and the library, there may be a supporting need for community interaction and the provision of special equipment and services. As you can see, there are no facile answers to the question, How much space is enough? (See Number 11 in the bibliography for further discussion.)

How To Use This Guide

- From the "menu" of areas, functions, and items, select the necessary ones needed to match the size of, type of, or program for the library being planned. The Universal Building Blocks section lists items or spaces common to many library functions (e.g., queuing space needed in circulation, reference, or photocopying), and these items therefore are not repeated under the other headings.
- Remember to include everything needed for a function and estimate the space accordingly; for example, a photocopying area might include the machine itself plus a sorting table, a paper recycling bin, and shelves for the reshelving of materials plus a debit card dispenser.
- For each item, multiply the number required by the amount of space given for each.
- The number of square feet needed for any general functional area will be the total space for items of furniture and equipment assigned to that heading. Where equipment is grouped in close proximity, some reduction in the given space requirement is advisable because the circulation space may be reduced.
- A worksheet for this purpose may be useful:

Example:
General Area: Library Instruction

No. of Items		square feet per item		minimum square footage required for functional space
2 computer stations	×	36 sq.ft.	=	72 sq.ft.
25 student seats	×	20 sq.ft.	=	500 sq.ft.

- The square-foot designations should be considered as building blocks; taken together these make up the basic needs for assigned spaces that would be included in the plan for the library project. Under "Square Feet Required Per Area or Item," space has been incorporated for an operator or user and an equipment-specific circulation area.
- Illustrative scale drawings follow the square-footage list.

Universal Building Blocks

Items and spaces listed here are common to many functional areas; consult this section when determining space required for specific functions.

	Required Per Area or Item	
	Square Feet	*Square Meters*
Book truck parking	8	0.743
Computer stations		
Terminal, work surface, chair (Illus. 6)	36	3.345
Terminal, work suface, chair with printer (Illus. 7)	45.5	4.181
Printer (networked)	36	3.345
Conference/meeting room	20/person (150 min.)	1.858/person
Add 15% of total for storage, if needed. If lobby is adjacent, add 20% of meeting room space for lobby.		
Filing cabinet (lateral)	15	1.394
Lockers (i.e., one full-height or two half-height, etc.)	5	0.465
Materials and supplies storage For items that require permanent storage space include storage space/rooms as necessary.		
Gurney/bin	16	1.486
Pallet/skid	12	1.115
Storage/supply cabinet (2 doors)	20	1.858
Supply room (see Admin./Staff)		
Photocopying/fax (Illus. 3)		
Machine, standard cabinet mounted (with or without coin op)	52	4.831
Station (machine, table, shelf, supplies, recycle containers) (Illus. 3)	80	7.432
Queuing area	9/person	0.836/person
Recycling container	6	0.557
Restrooms—for public or staff see local codes; include in non-assignable space		
Tables		
Two seat (nose-to-nose)	40/person	3.716/person
Four seat (youth or adult) (Illus. 4)	30/person	2.787/person
Workstation (Illus. 5) (includes terminal, printer, work surface, chair, file, shelving, guest chair)	84.8	7.886

Shelving and Media Storage
Shelving Matrix (Illus. 12)

		Base Shelf		
Aisle Width	*10 inches*	*12 inches*	*15 inches*	*18 inches*
36 inches	8.75 sq. ft.	9.40 sq. ft.	10.30 sq. ft.	11.25 sq. ft.
42 inches	9.70 sq. ft.	10.30 sq. ft.	11.25 sq. ft.	12.20 sq. ft.
48 inches	10.65 sq. ft.	11.25 sq. ft.	12.20 sq. ft.	13.15 sq. ft.

Library shelving constitutes the largest single allocation of space in a conventional library. The floor space required by an individual shelving unit is determined by a combination of the width of the shelving unit, the depth of the unit, and the width of the aisle found in the bookstack. The above chart provides an estimate of floor space required per shelving unit in different shelving environments. The chart assumes a standard 36-inch shelving width. To determine the appropriate space allocation for a given shelving environment, read across from the desired aisle width to the desired base shelf depth. For example, a collection housed on shelving 36 inches wide and 12 inches deep installed on a 42-inch aisle requires 10.30 square feet *per single-faced unit of shelving.* For double-faced shelving units, multiply the space allocation on this table by two. For metric conversion, multiply each number by .093.

Video Storage
Use matrix for shelving according to individual manufacturer for shelf base (average 12 inches/unit.)

CD or CD-ROM Storage
See page 7 if using storage cabinets, or use matrix for shelving according to shelf base.

Spinners for Paperbacks, CDs, CD-ROMs, Cassettes, Videos, Etc.

	Square Ft.	*Square Meters*
Per unit (Illus. 14) (30-inch base diameter)	42.25/unit	3.925/unit

Compact Shelving

	Square Ft.	*Square Meters*
Single-faced, 10-inch base	3.75/unit	0.348/unit

In closed stacks, every fifth or sixth range must be immovable (fixed); in open stacks, every third or fourth range, according to frequency of use. The more use, the more fixed ranges for ease of use. Figure these according to the shelving matrix so there will be aisle space.

Note: Compact shelving requires additional floor load—about 300 lbs./sq. ft.; the normal floor load for a library is about 150 lbs./sq. ft. Refer to your structural engineer for floor load requirements.

Public and Specialized User Areas

	Required Per Area or Item	
	Square Feet	*Square Meters*
Carrel		
Adult, youth, undergraduate (Illus. 6 and 7)	36–45.5	3.345–4.273
Faculty study (enclosed) (Illus. 8)	80	7.432
Graduate student (Illus. 9) (includes lockable storage bin, filing space, terminal, work surface)	63	5.853
Children's area Spaces given here accommodate the way in which children approach and use furniture, equipment, etc.		
Child's lounge seat	36	3.345
Child's table (4-place)	90	8.361
Floor activity space	20/person	1.858/person
Service desk	120/staff station	11.148/staff station
Storytelling/multipurpose area	15/child	1.394/child
Circulation checkout (see also Circulation under Non-Public for staff space)		
Self-checkout	45.5/station	4.227/station
Display area		
Display rack (wall mounted)	9	0.836
Handout display rack, free-standing	20	1.858
"New Book" display (free-standing, all types)	50	4.645
Faculty study (see Carrel)		
Graduate workstation (see Carrel)		
Information/reference or interlibrary loan area		
Atlas/folio case (free-standing) (Illus. 1)	36.75	3.414
Borrowing station (ILL)	40	3.716
Card catalog (60-drawer unit, single-faced, free-standing)	20	1.858
CD-ROM station (Illus. 7) (includes printer)	45.5	4.227
CD-ROM storage	15	1.394
Dictionary stand	25	2.322
Index table	150	13.935
Information desk	40/staff station	3.716/staff station
Office (Head of Reference—see Non-Public Areas)		
Online search station (PC, printer, manuals, etc.: space for 2 people to confer, e.g., searcher and patron)	100/station	9.290/station

	Required Per Area or Item	
	Square Feet	*Square Meters*
Patron access catalog		
without printer (Illus. 6)	36	3.345
with printer (Illus. 7)	45.5	
Reference service desk (includes interview and equipment space)	120/staff station	11.148/staff station
Library instruction/user education area		
Equipment storage (to be stored, e.g., overhead projector with or without cart)	6/unit	0.557/unit
Instructor's space (incl. circulation area and console)	118	10.963
Podium	12.5	1.161
Projection screen (6-foot-wide free-standing)	48	4.459
Student seating (tablet arm classroom seating)	20	1.858
Light table/map viewing	56	5.203
Listening areas		
Individual (Illus. 6)	36-45.5	4.181
Group (good for both large and small groups)	15/person	1.394/person
Lobby (if separate)—Add 20% of meeting room space		
Lobby and entrance area		
Bench (free-standing)	36	3.345
Public or emergency telephone		
Wall-mounted	10	0.929
Free-standing	16	1.486
Guards desk	24	2.230
Security system (typically 4 feet × 6 feet per aisle) (vestibule site specific, included in nonassignable area)	24	2.230
Lounge seat (Illus. 10 and 11)	32-68/seat	2.973-6.317/seat
Map viewing station—see Light table		
Media/Publications center		
Audio recording room	120	11.148
Audio studio	150	13.935
Classroom	30/person	2.787/person
Conference room	30/person	2.787/person
Darkroom	80	7.432
Editing	80	7.432
Equipment manuals	10/shelving unit	0.929/shelving unit
Equipment station—see Bibliographic instruction area		
Graphics (computer-generated)	50	4.645

| | Required Per Area or Item | |
	Square Feet	Square Meters
Preview room	50	4.645
Production workstation	120	11.148
Repair/cleaning workstation	80	7.432
Reproduction (workstation)	80	7.432
Slide viewing station (includes projection screen)	56	5.203
Storage	15% of total space	15% of total space
TV studio	1,200	111.484
TV studio, small	600	55.742
Microcomputer laboratory		
Microcomputer lab station (Illus. 7) (includes terminal, printer, work surface, manuals)	45.5	4.227
Microcomputer lab service desk	120/staff station	11.148/staff station
Microform equipment		
Microfilm/fiche reader	36	3.345
Microfilm/fiche reader/printer	36	3.345
Microfilm/fiche reader/printer with tablet arms (Illus. 15)	61.75	5.742
Film/fiche duplicator (hot processor, no drying cabinet)	80	7.432
Microform storage (multipurpose film or fiche cabinet)		
single-faced (includes access/aisle)	18	1.672
double-faced	36	3.345
Periodicals display—see Stack or Display entries (Number of units required is dependent upon number of titles to be shelved and how densely titles are to be displayed.)		
Study room (for group work) (illus. 13)	30/person	2.787/person
Administration/Staff		
Coat storage	8/person	0.716/person
Offices		
Director (includes desk, credenza, guest seating, bookcase)	200	18.580
Other	150	13.935
Supervisor workstation	120	11.148
Kitchen	80	7.432
Kitchenette	50	4.645
Reception area	20/person	1.858/person
Restroom, executive	30	2.787
Safe (2.5-feet square)	6	0.557

	Required Per Area or Item	
	Square Feet	*Square Meters*
Staff supply room	120 minimum	11.148
Work/sorting table	40	3.716
Bindery conservation:		
Binding equipment (normally part of staff workstation)	10	0.929
Board cutter	85/60 in.blade	215.9/152.5cm
Book press	15	1.393
Paper cutter	50/36 in. blade	127/91.44cm blade
Roller backer	20	1.858
Shipping boxes	8/stack	0.743/stack
Tying machine	25	2.322
Stamper	20	1.858
Bookmobile and outreach area	Equipment and site specific	

Non-Public and Professional/Staff Work Areas

	Required Per Area or Item	
	Square Feet	*Square Meters*
Circulation control area		
This is staff space; for public space, see Circulation checkout on page 7.		
Book sensitization workstation (free standing)	40	3.716
Book return unit		
Free-standing	16	1.486
As part of counter	12	1.115
Circ. desk, online single station (includes terminal and desensitization unit)	80	7.432
Circ. desk, manual, small	120	11.148
Patron transaction space	25/station	2.322/station
Sorting/staging area	20/unit of shelving	1.858/unit of shelving
Computer room		
Computer terminal	6	0.557
Console, operators	20	1.858
CPU	42	3.901
Disk drives, external	42	3.901
Environmental controls—See manufacturer's requirements		
Fire-suppression equipment—See manufacturer's requirements		
Power supply, uninterruptable	10	0.929
Printer	36	3.345
Storage	Equipment and site specific	
Tape drive, external	30	2.787
Telecommunications equipment	20	1.858
Copy service—see specific items		
Mail/Receiving		
Dumpster	86	7.990
Flat truck	16	1.486
Hand truck	4	0.372
Loading dock (minimum 1 truck)	110	10.219
Mail hampers	9	0.836
Scale	6	0.557
Sorting table	40	3.716
Stapler, foot operated	6	0.557
Tape dispensers	2	0.186
Bag rack	11	1.021

	Required Per Area or Item	
	Square Feet	*Square Meters*
Wrapping table	33	3.066
Weighing/metering counter	33	3.066
Mail delivery cart	15	1.394
Maintenance office and area		
Facility manager (includes desk, plan file, drafting table, chairs, files, bookcases)	200	18.580
Repair room (includes workbench, tool and equipment storage)	150	13.935
Technical Services—see specific items elsewhere		

Illustration 1. Atlas Stand—Axonometric

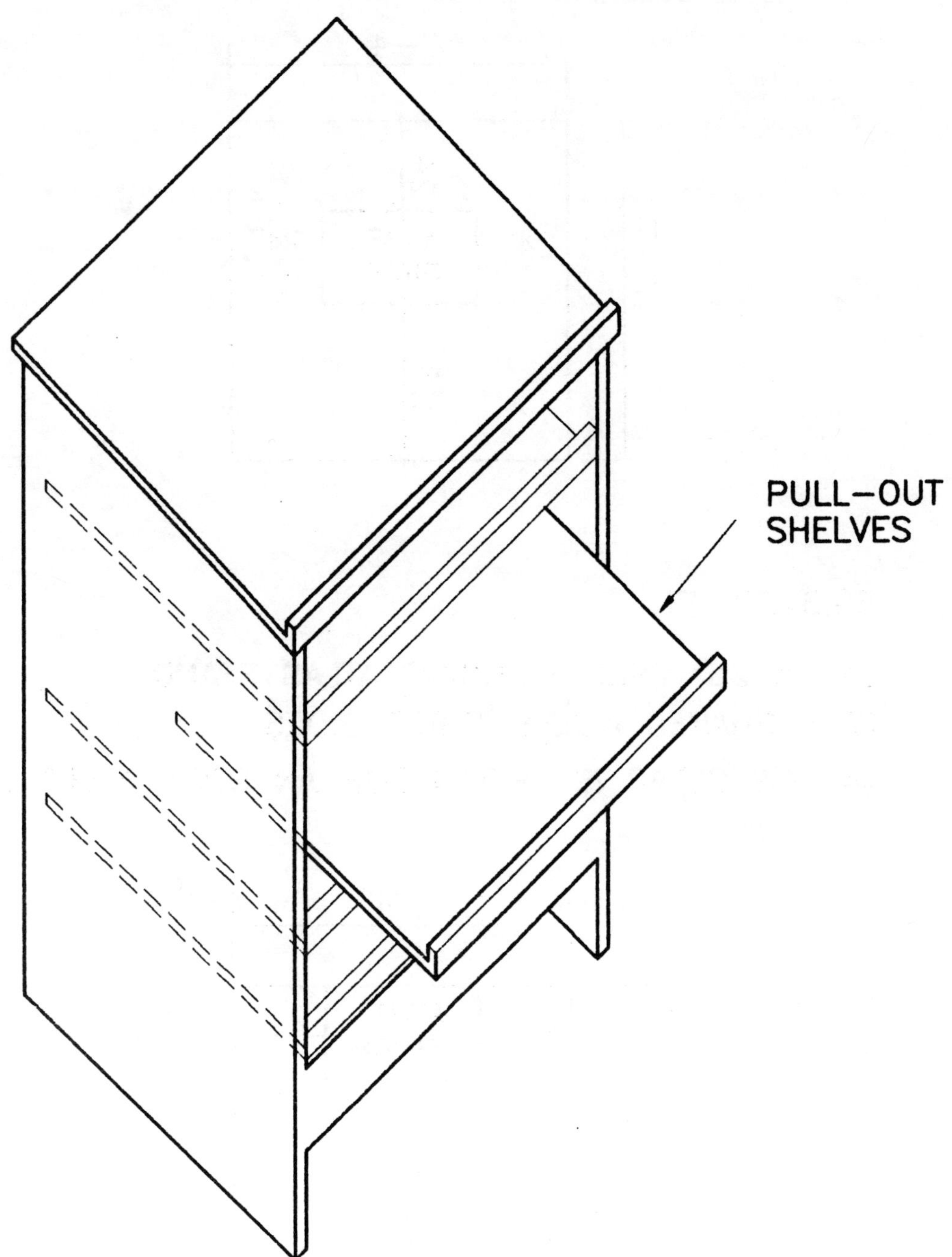

Illustration 2. Atlas Stand

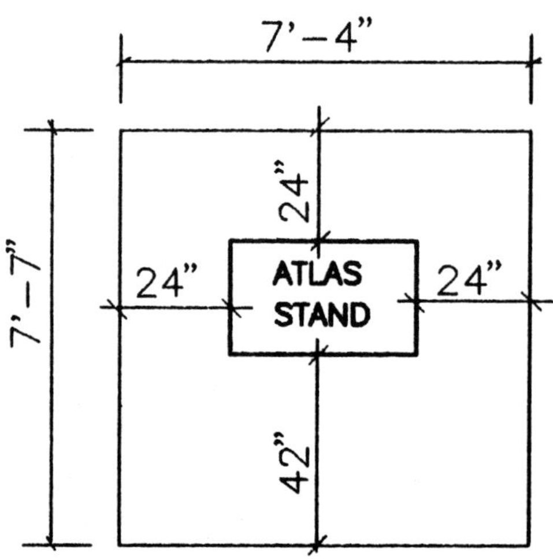

55.3 SQ. FT.

31" X 25" FREE STANDING ATLAS STAND
WITH SHARED AISLES THREE SIDES
(40" W CLEAR IS SHOWN FOR AN OPEN ATLAS ON TOP)

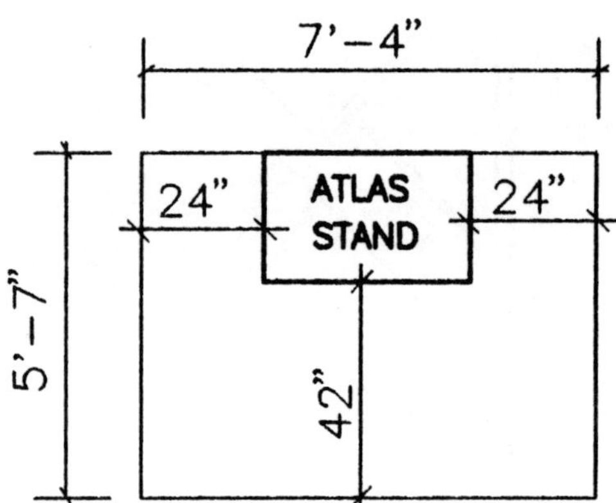

40.7 SQ. FT.

31" X 25" FREE STANDING ATLAS STAND
WITH SHARED AISLES TWO SIDES
(40" W CLEAR IS SHOWN FOR AN OPEN ATLAS ON TOP)

Illustration 3. Coin/Card–Op Photocopier/Fax

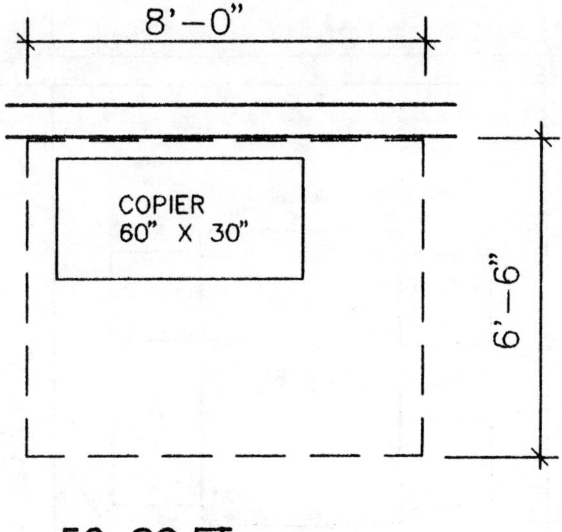

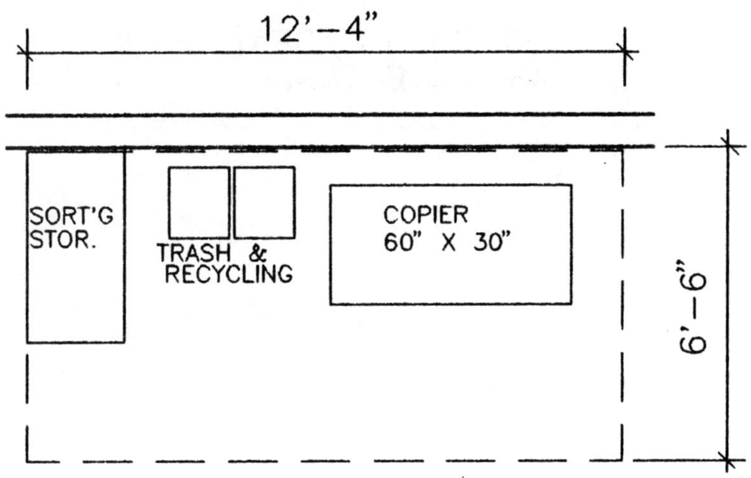

Illustration 4. Reading Table

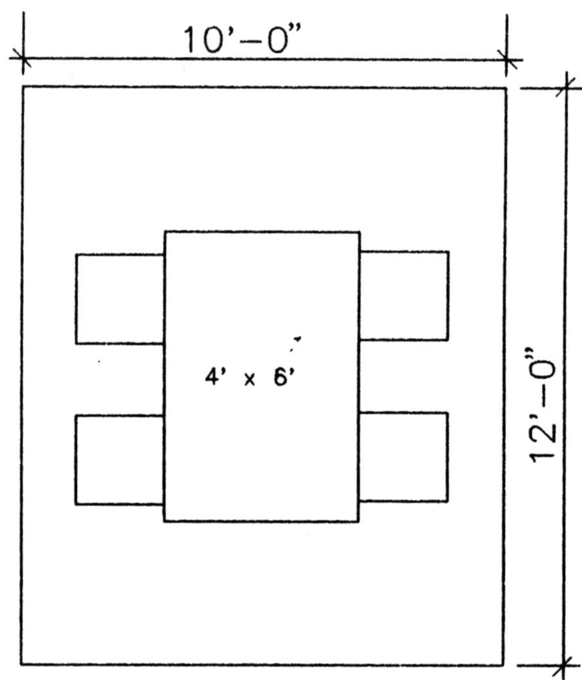

Illustration 5. Staff Workstations

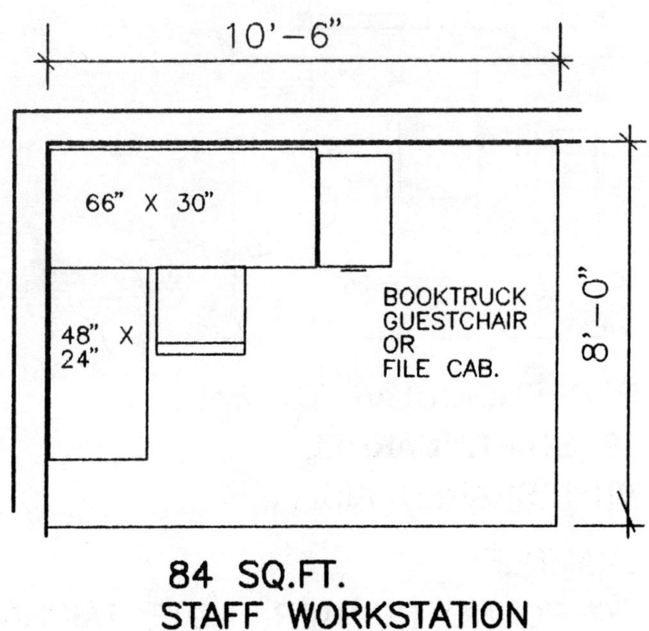

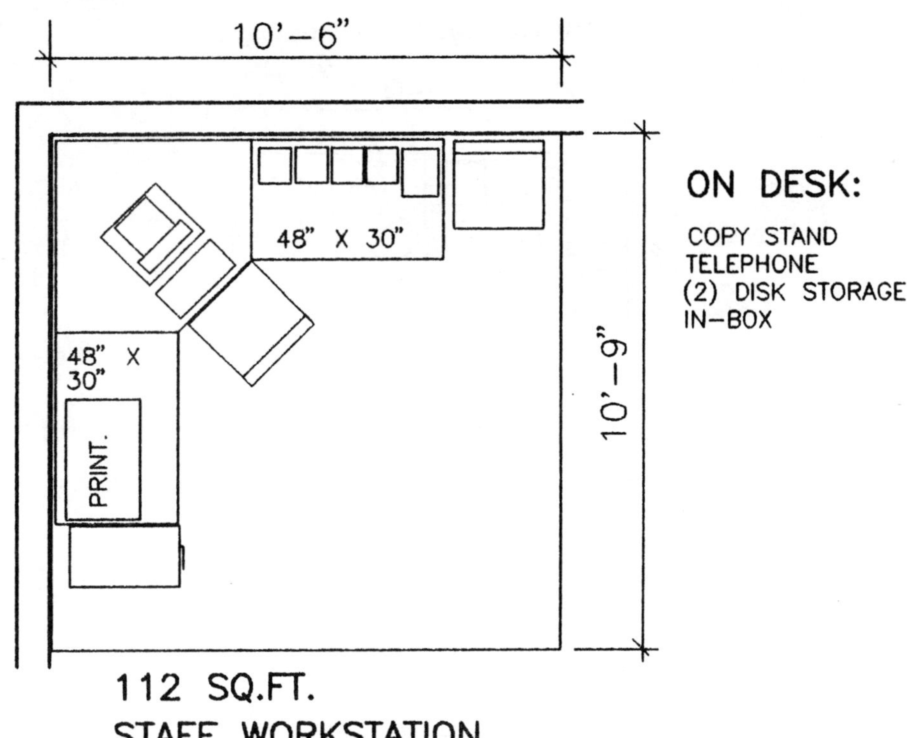

Illustration 6. Staff Workstation

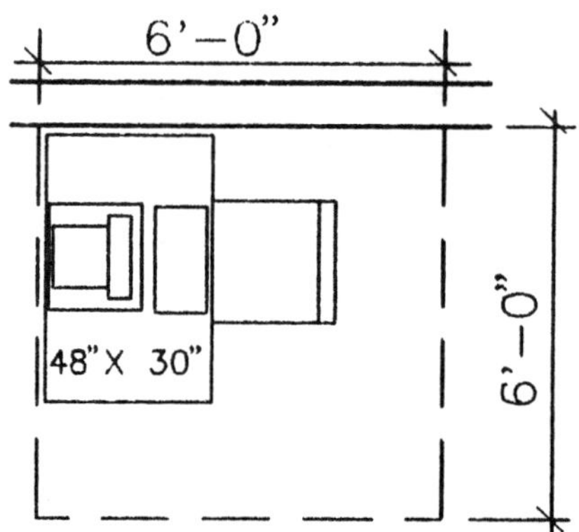

PERPENDICULAR TO WALL
36 SQ.FT. CARREL
WITH SHARED AISLES

EXAMPLE:

- PC NO PRINTER, NOTE TAKING
  SPACE LIMITED
- LISTENING UNIT
- OPAC WITH SMALL PRINTER

Illustration 7. Technology Station

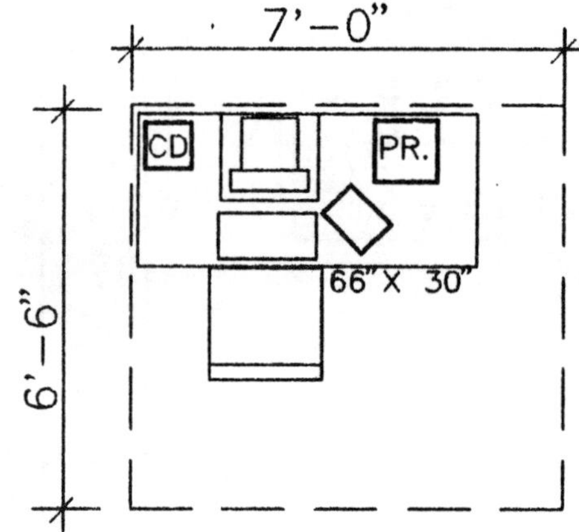

FACING WALL
45.5 SQ.FT. CARREL
WITH SHARED AISLES

EXAMPLE:

- PC WITH PRINTER AND MOUSE,
  SPACE FOR NOTE TAKING
- CD ROM DRIVE AND MULTI MEDIA
- OPAC WITH PRINTER, MOUSE
- MICROCOMPUTER LAB STATION
- LARGE LISTENING AREA

Illustration 8. Faculty Study

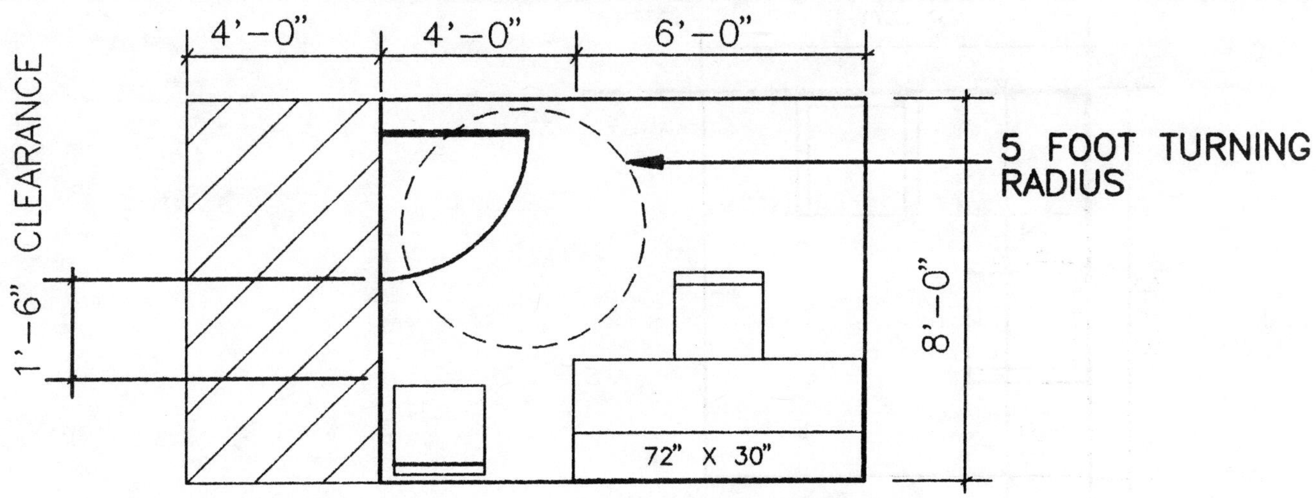

80 SQ.FT.
FACULTY STUDY   (NOTE: 112 S.F. INCLUDING AISLE SPACE)

Illustration 9. Graduate Carrel

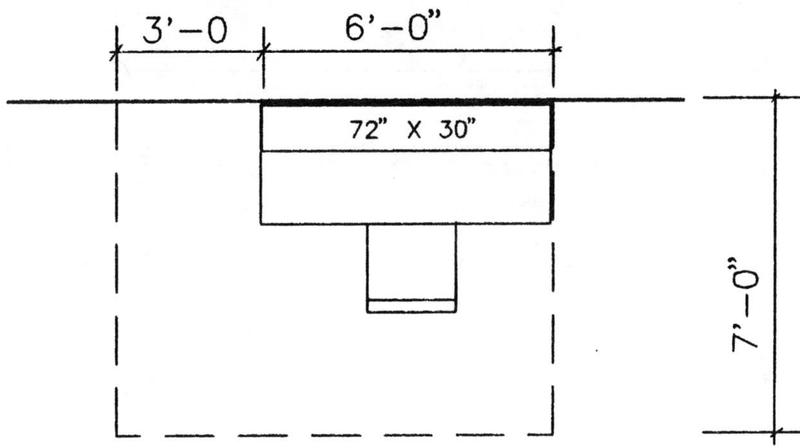

63 SQ.FT.
GRADUATE CARREL

Illustration 10. Lounge Seating

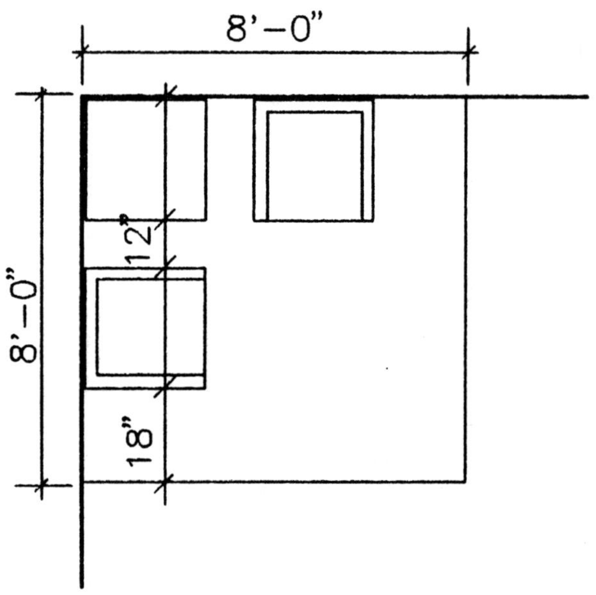

64 SQ.FT. DIVIDED BY 2 = 32 SQ.FT. PER SEAT
(USING 30" X 30" CHAIRS)

Illustration 11. Lounge Seating—Social Distance

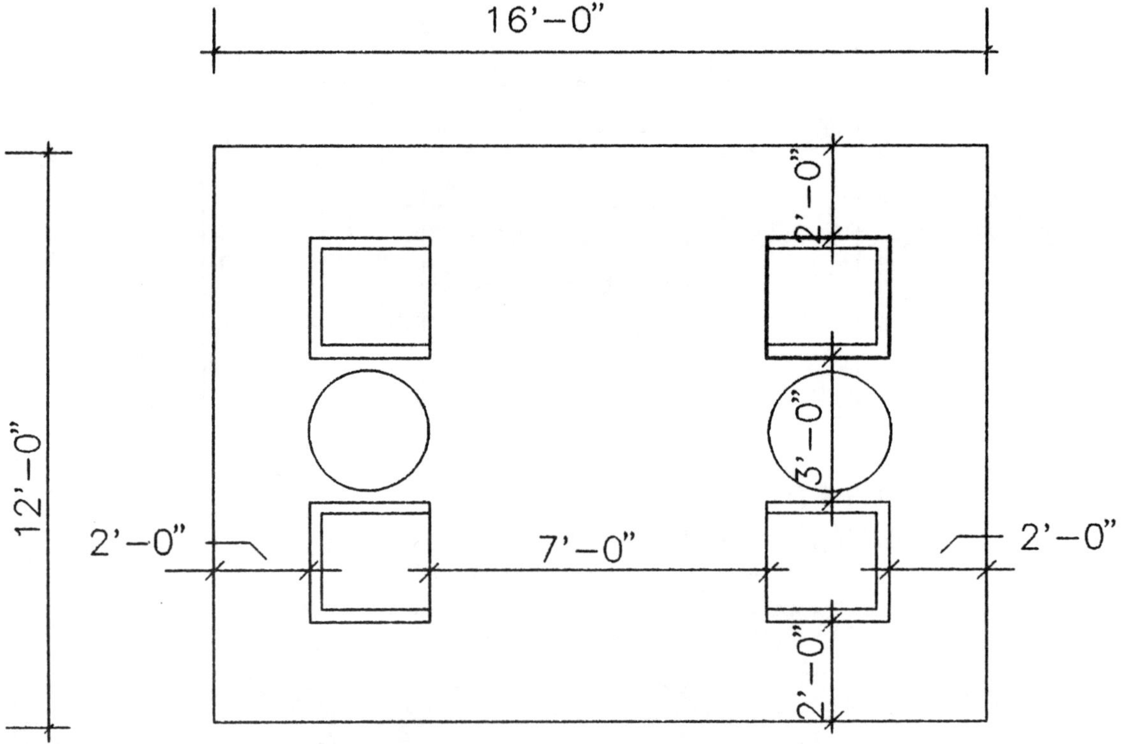

192 SQ.FT. DIVIDED BY 4 = 48 SQ.FT. PER SEAT
(USING 30" X 30" CHAIRS)

Illustration 12. Standard Steel Bracket Shelving

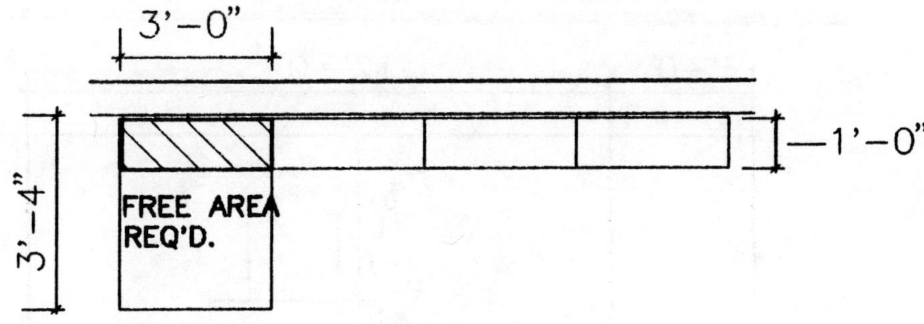

10 SQ. FT. PER ONE
SINGLE—FACE SECTION
AT WALL

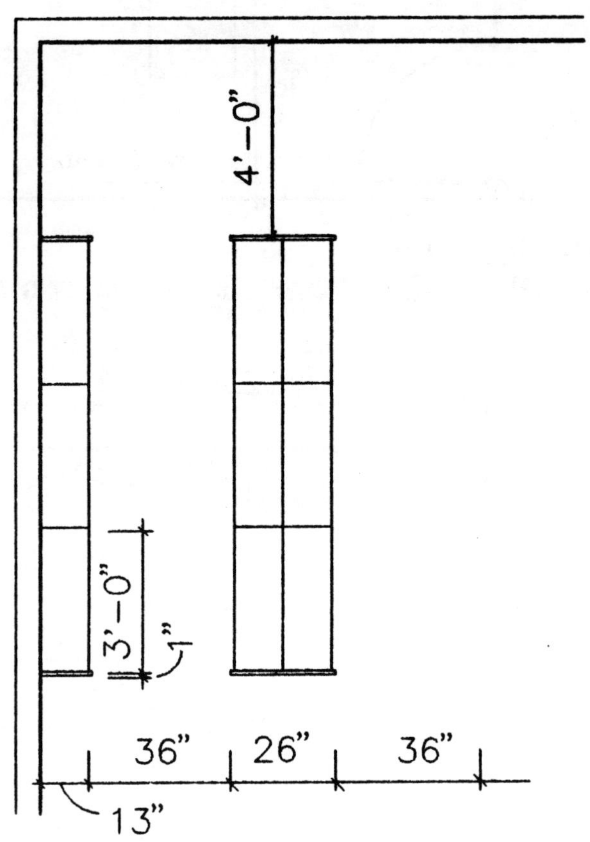

13" (SINGLE FACE BASE
AND END PANEL)

SINGLE & DOUBLE FACED
UNITS.

Illustration 13. Two Group Study Layouts

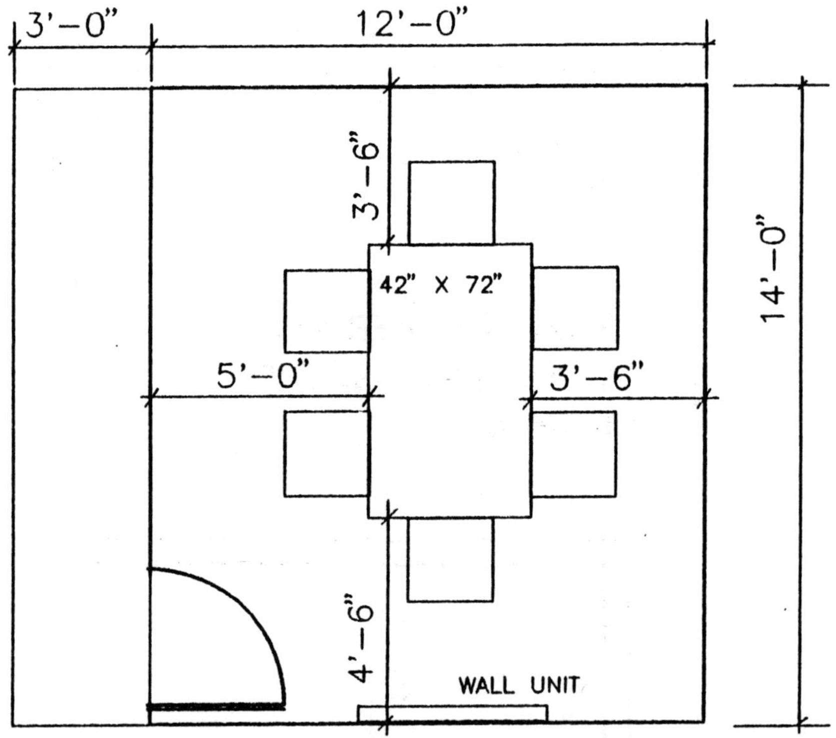

168 SQ. FT.
GROUP STUDY? (NOTE: 210 S.F. INCLUDING AISLE SPACE)

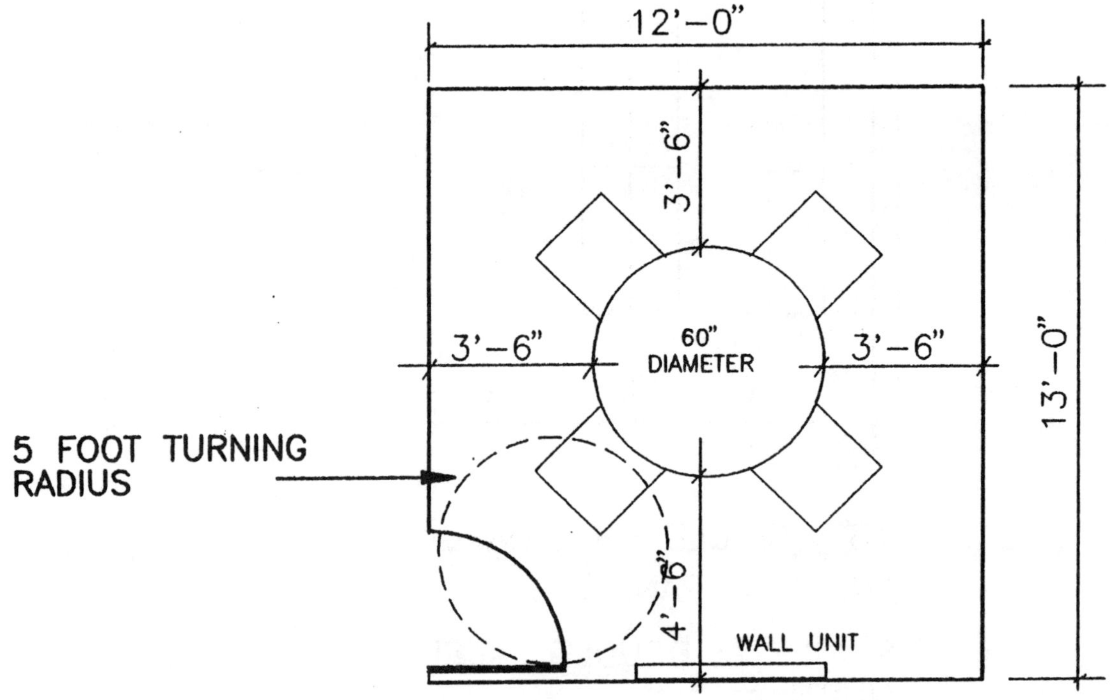

156 SQ. FT.
GROUP STUDY WITH ROUND TABLE

Illustration 14. Spinner

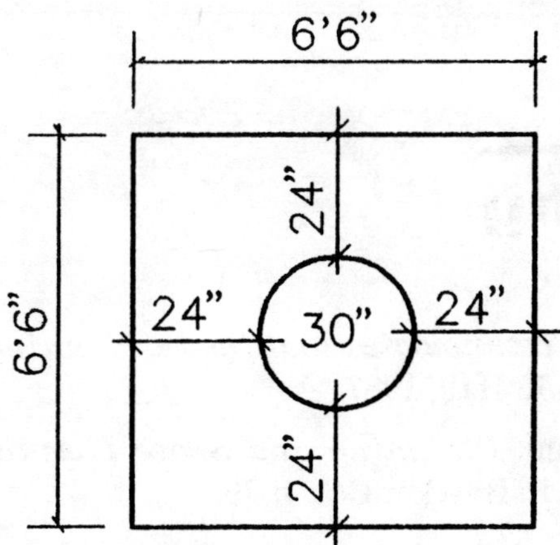

42.25 SQ. FT.

**30" DIAMETER BASE
SPINNING CD, CD ROM,
CASSETTE, VIDEO CASSETTE HOLDER?
WITH SHARED AISLES ALL SIDES**

Illustration 15. Microform Reader

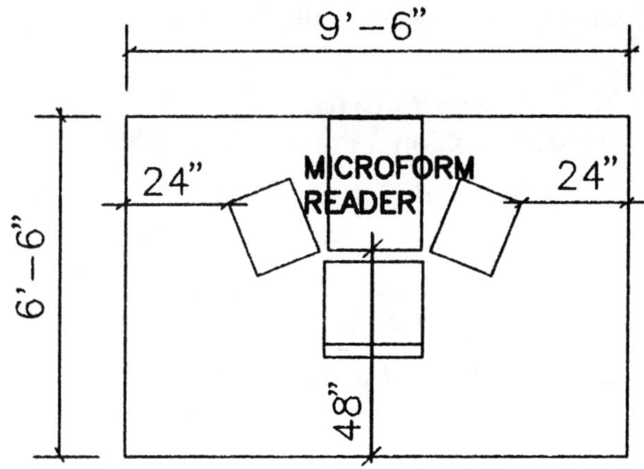

61.75 SQ. FT.

**MICROFORM READER/PRINTER WITH TABLET ARMS
SHARED AISLES THREE SIDES**

Brief Bibliography

1. Boss, Richard W. *Information Technologies and Space Planning for Libraries and Information Centers.* Boston: G.K. Hall, 1987.

2. Cohen, Aaron, and Elaine Cohen. *Designing and Space Planning for Libraries: A Behavioral Guide.* New York: R.R. Bowker Co., 1979.

3. Cohen, Elaine, and Aaron Cohen. *Automation, Space Management, and Productivity: A Guide for Libraries.* New York: R.R. Bowker Co., 1982.

4. Dahlgren, Anders C., and Erla P. Heyns, comps. *Planning Library Buildings: A Select Bibliography.* 4th ed. Chicago: Library Administration and Management Association, American Library Association, 1995.

5. Dahlgren, Anders C. *Public Library Space Needs: A Planning Outline.* Madison, Wisc.: Department of Public Instruction, 1988.

6. Fraley, Ruth A., and Carol Lee Anderson. *Library Space Planning: A How-To-Do-It Manual for Assessing, Allocating, and Reorganizing Collections, Resources, and Facilities.* 2d ed. New York: Neal-Schuman Publishers, 1990.

7. Freifeld, Roberta, and Acryl Masyr. *Space Planning.* Washington, D.C.: Special Libraries Association, 1991.

8. Kennedy, Gail, ed. and comp. *Library Buildings Consultant List, 1995.* Chicago: Library Administration and Management Association, American Library Association, 1995.

9. Lushington, Nolan, and Willis N. Mills, Jr. *Libraries Designed for Users: A Planning Handbook.* Hamden, Conn.: Library Professional Publications, 1980.

10. Metcalf, Keyes, D. *Planning Academic and Research Library Buildings.* 2d ed. by Leighton, Philip D. and David C. Weber. Chicago: American Library Association, 1986.

11. Michaels, Andrea, and David. "Breakthrough Facility Planning for New Libraries: How Much Space is Enough?" *Encyclopedia of Library and Information Science.* Vol. 57, 1995.

12. Sannwald, William W., ed. *Checklist of Library Building Design Considerations.* 2d ed. Chicago: Library Administration and Management Association, 1991.

13. Weihs, Jean Riddle. *The Integrated Library: Encouraging Access to Multimedia Materials.* 2d ed. Phoenix, Ariz.: Oryx Press, 1991.

Note: The present work takes into account current ADA, life safety, and information technology considerations. Although the works cited in this bibliography may not be current in all of these regards, they contain general discussions of space planning which remain useful.